ESSENTIAL LIBRARY OF SOCIAL CHANGE

WOMEN'S RIGHTS MOVEMENT

ABDO
Publishing Company

ESSENTIAL LIBRARY OF SOCIAL CHANGE

WOMEN'S RIGHTS MOVEMENT

by Jennifer Joline Anderson

Content Consultant

Arzoo Osanloo, JD, PhD
Law, Societies, and Justice Program
University of Washington

CREDITS

Published by ABDO Publishing Company, PO Box 398166, Minneapolis, MN 55439. Copyright © 2014 by Abdo Consulting Group, Inc. International copyrights reserved in all countries. No part of this book may be reproduced in any form without written permission from the publisher. The Essential Library™ is a trademark and logo of ABDO Publishing Company.

Printed in the United States of America,
North Mankato, Minnesota
062013
092013

 THIS BOOK CONTAINS AT LEAST 10% RECYCLED MATERIALS.

Editor: Angela Wiechmann
Series Designer: Emily Love

Photo credits: Library of Congress, cover, 2, 9, 16, 28 (left), 28 (right), 33, 37, 45; Bettmann/Corbis/AP Images, 6, 48, 54, 57, 58, 67; North Wind/ North Wind Picture Archives, 18, 21, 39; Wilbur & Orville Wright/Library of Congress, 26; Fotosearch/Stringer/Getty Images, 40; Harris & Ewing/ Library of Congress, 50; Howard R. Hollem/Library of Congress, 62; Don Carl Steffen/Gamma-Rapho/Getty Images, 68, 72; Fred W. McDarrah/Getty Images, 77; Paul Sakuma/AP Images, 78; Jennifer Law/AFP/Getty Images, 83; Ebet Roberts/Redferns/Getty Images, 87; Charles Krupa/AP Images, 88; Scott Olson/Getty Images, 93; Shutterstock Images, 97

Library of Congress Control Number: 2013932970

Cataloging-in-Publication Data

Anderson, Jennifer Joline.
 Women's rights movement / Jennifer Joline Anderson.
  p. cm. -- (Essential library of social change)
Includes bibliographical references and index.
ISBN 978-1-61783-889-7
1. Women--Social conditions--Juvenile literature. 2. Women--Economic conditions--Juvenile literature. I. Title.
305.42--dc23

2013932970

CONTENTS

CHAPTER 1

A REVOLUTION BEGINS

It was the morning of July 19, 1848. In Seneca Falls, New York, a historic gathering was about to take place—the first women's rights convention. But event organizers Lucretia Mott and Elizabeth Cady Stanton were worried. Local farming families were busy with the haying season. Would anyone take the time to come to a discussion about women's rights?

As Stanton's horse-drawn cart made its way toward Wesleyan Chapel, where the meeting was set to take place, she saw wagon after wagon coming down the street. Women were coming from all over the county. Some were in fancy carriages, and some were on foot. Some were fine ladies. Some were farm women. Some were factory workers who had taken time off without pay to attend the two-day event. Old and young, rich and poor, women were coming together to talk about their rights. By the time they reached the chapel, they formed a crowd of approximately 300 people. Among them were 40 men, including the famous abolitionist and former slave Frederick Douglass.[1]

THE STATE OF WOMEN'S RIGHTS

All these women—and men, too—had come to stand up for women's rights. Women in the 1800s held very few of the rights they enjoy today. Married women could not own property. Even the wages they earned and the clothes on their backs legally belonged to their husbands. In a divorce, children belonged to the father. Colleges and universities would not admit women. Educators believed women's brains were too small to handle rigorous academics. Women were not allowed to participate in sports, either. They were supposedly too weak for heavy exercise. Women could hold few jobs besides housekeeper, elementary schoolteacher, or farm or factory worker. Female doctors, lawyers, and politicians were unknown. On top of it all, women could not vote, so they had no political power to help change the way society treated them.

Stanton was well aware of these injustices. The daughter of a judge, young Elizabeth had seen desperate women come to her father's law office seeking help. But most of the time, there was nothing Stanton's father could do. The laws simply did not recognize women as having the same rights as men. As a young child, Elizabeth thought she could change the unfair laws simply by cutting them out of her father's law books. But her father stopped her. "When you are grown up, and able to prepare a speech, you must . . . talk to

"I WISH YOU WERE A BOY!"

Elizabeth Cady Stanton grew up in a mansion in Johnstown, New York. Her father, Daniel Cady, was a judge and a wealthy, important man. The pride of the family was Elizabeth's older brother, Eleazer. But a few weeks after graduating from college, Eleazer fell ill and died. Judge Cady was devastated. Elizabeth, age 11, tried to comfort her father. "Oh, my daughter," he said, "I wish you were a boy!"[2]

Elizabeth resolved to prove a daughter could be as good as a son. She studied hard, learned Latin and Greek, and mastered horseback riding. And still her father said, "You should have been a boy."[3] She was never able to change her father's mind about girls. But as a talented writer, speaker, and thinker who dedicated her life to women's rights, Stanton helped changed many minds—and laws—across the nation.

From the time she was a young girl, Stanton, seen here with her daughter Harriot, felt compelled to stand up for women's rights.

the legislators; tell them all you have seen in this office."[4] Elizabeth vowed she would do just that.

TIME TO TAKE A STAND

The 1840s were an exciting time in the United States—a time of change and reform. Stanton and her husband, Henry, were active in the abolition movement, fighting to end slavery. Stanton felt a connection with African Americans trapped in bondage. In a way, she thought, all women were like slaves. They had been denied their full freedom. The time felt right for women of all races to unite and demand their full rights as citizens of the United States.

In July 1848, Stanton met with Mott, her friend and fellow abolitionist, and a group of other women. As they poured cups of tea, the women poured out their anger and frustration over the injustices American women faced. They made a plan to hold a women's rights convention the very next week.

That Friday, a notice appeared in the newspaper:

WOMAN'S RIGHTS CONVENTION. *A Convention to discuss the social, civil, and religious condition and rights of woman will be held in the Wesleyan Chapel, at Seneca Falls, N. Y., on Wednesday and Thursday, the 19th and 20th of July, current; commencing at 10 o'clock A. M. During the first day the meeting will be exclusively for women, who are earnestly invited to attend. The public generally are invited to be present on the second day, when Lucretia Mott, of Philadelphia, and other ladies and gentlemen, will address the Convention.*[5]

The notice likely shocked many readers. Conventions organized by women were not unusual. But a meeting about women's rights was unheard of. The idea that both women and men would be speaking at the gathering was shocking, too. Women rarely spoke in front of an audience that included men. To do so was considered unwomanly and immoral.

A NEW DECLARATION OF INDEPENDENCE

Now that they had called a meeting, the convention organizers needed to prepare a statement about the goals they hoped to accomplish. It was Stanton's idea to model their statement after the US Declaration of Independence. Their Declaration of Sentiments read that "all men and women are created equal."[6] The declaration continued with a long list of complaints women had about the way men treated them. Representing all men and women as "he" and "she," respectively, the declaration claimed,

> He has endeavored, in every way that he could

LUCRETIA MOTT

Lucretia Coffin Mott, a native of Massachusetts, was raised in the Quaker faith. Quakers, unlike other religious groups of the time, allowed women to fully participate in the church. Mott became a Quaker minister. With her husband, James, she traveled across the country speaking against slavery. The Motts even refused to use sugar and cotton, as these were produced by slave labor. Mott met Stanton at the World's Anti-Slavery Convention in London, England, in 1840. Stanton admired Mott, and the two began a lifelong friendship.

to destroy her confidence in her own powers,
to lessen her self-respect, and to make her
willing to lead a dependent and abject life.[7]

Along with the declaration was a list of 11 resolutions, or statements, of what the women believed should be done to resolve the complaints. A key resolution was "Resolved, That woman is man's equal—was intended to be so by the Creator, and the highest good of the race demands that she should be recognized as such."[8]

A HEATED DEBATE

On July 19, the first day of the Seneca Falls Convention, Stanton read the declaration aloud. The next day, all who gathered were asked to vote on the resolutions. After some discussion, the first eight resolutions were unanimously approved. But then, they reached the ninth resolution, which stated women must seek the right to vote: "Resolved, That it is the duty of the women of this country to secure to themselves their sacred right to the elective franchise."[9] The convention erupted in a heated debate.

Stanton had known this resolution would be the most controversial. In 1848, women's suffrage was a radical topic. The general public believed women had no place in the political sphere. Many convention members did think women should be allowed to vote. But they worried pushing for voting rights might turn the public against the convention and everything else the members stood for. Rather, some argued, they should seek reform in other areas and leave voting rights for another time. Even Mott was against the resolution, telling Stanton, "Why, Lizzie, thee will make us ridiculous."[10]

But Stanton argued passionately for women's right to vote. After all, she said, even "drunkards . . . horse-racing rum-selling rowdies" and "silly boys" had the right to vote. To her, that was an insult. "The right is ours. Have it we must. Use it we will," she insisted.[11]

Just when it seemed the resolution would not pass, a man in the crowd stood up. It was Frederick Douglass, the former slave and abolitionist who was famous for his powerful speeches. Douglass spoke strongly in support of the voting rights resolution. There could be no freedom without the vote, he argued, either for African Americans or for women of any race. He stated,

FREDERICK DOUGLASS

Douglass was born a slave in 1818 and escaped to freedom in 1838. For the rest of his life, he spoke out against slavery and racism. His book *Narrative of the Life of Frederick Douglass* became a best seller and helped the abolition movement. Douglass was a powerful supporter of women's rights, too. If women were denied the right to vote, he pointed out, "not merely the degradation of woman and the perpetuation of a great injustice happens, but the maiming and repudiation of one-half of the moral and intellectual power of the government of the world."[12]

"The power to choose rulers and make laws was the right by which all others could be secured."[13]

After Douglass spoke, the convention voted again on the resolution, and it passed. In total, 68 women and 32 men signed their names to the Declaration of Sentiments and Resolutions.[14] That evening, the convention concluded with a moving speech by Mott. The attendees walked out into the summer night feeling the meeting had been a triumph.

"SHOCKING AND UNNATURAL"

Not everyone in the general public agreed, however. The convention was ridiculed in newspapers. One article described the meeting as "the most shocking and unnatural incident ever recorded in the history of womanity."[15] An article in a Philadelphia, Pennsylvania, paper complained that women should be modest and discreet, not "standing out for woman's rights." The writer added, "A woman is nobody. A wife is everything."[16] Only a few newspapers, such as Douglass's *North Star*, supported the women.

Amid the controversy, many women who had signed the declaration were shamed into removing their names. But not Stanton. She noted that even though they criticized and mocked the convention, some of the newspapers had also printed the Declaration of

In her autobiography, *Eighty Years and More*, Stanton remembers the reaction of the press to the first women's rights convention:

"The convention . . . was in every way a grand success. . . . No words could express our astonishment on finding, a few days afterward, that what seemed to us so timely, so rational, and so sacred, should be a subject for sarcasm and ridicule to the entire press of the nation. . . . So pronounced was the popular voice against us, in the parlor, press, and pulpit, that most of the ladies who had attended the convention and signed the declaration, one by one, withdrew their names and influence and joined our persecutors. Our friends gave us the cold shoulder and felt themselves disgraced by the whole proceeding.

If I had had the slightest premonition of all that was to follow that convention, I fear I should not have had the courage to risk it. . . . But we had set the ball in motion." [17]

Sentiments. It was free publicity for the movement. "It will start women thinking, and men too," Stanton commented.[18]

Over the next several years, activists organized women's rights conventions in cities all over the nation. There would be a long road ahead for the women's rights movement. In all, 72 years would pass before women in the United States would win the right to vote in 1920. And more than 100 years after the convention, American women would still be fighting for the right to be treated equally to men. But a spark had been lit. ●

« Thanks to the eloquence of organizer Lucretia Mott, the convention at Seneca Falls would inspire women's rights activists for decades to come.

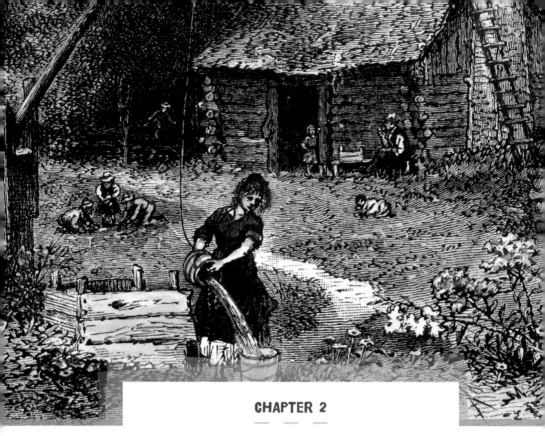

CHAPTER 2

EARLY AMERICAN WOMEN

W hen the first European settlers arrived in North America, they brought along their social values, customs, and attitudes. Among these was the belief that women were inherently inferior to men. Religious and political leaders taught that husbands should rule over their wives. According to John Winthrop, a Puritan leader and governor of Massachusetts Bay Colony in the 1630s, a man was "[his wife's] lord and she is to be subject to him."[1]

The marriage laws reflected this belief. Just as in Britain, a married woman in the American colonies could not sign contracts and could not own property. Instead, she and her children were considered her husband's property. In colonial days, women rarely received any education beyond learning to read the Bible and perform important household tasks. They were believed to be the "weaker sex," dependent upon men to lead them, and their place was in the home.

In reality, colonial women were anything but weak. The early settlers' life demanded hard, backbreaking work. Women worked alongside men to clear land for farming and plant crops. They had to grow all their own food and make their own soap

SALEM WITCH TRIALS

In 1692, more than 150 people were accused of witchcraft in Salem, Massachusetts. Of those, 19 were executed. Most were women.[2] Many of the accused women were unmarried or widowed, had no children, or in some way were outsiders to the community. Because they did not fit into society's ideal of proper womanhood, it was easy for people to label them as immoral. The witch trials were a tragic example of rigid Puritan values in colonial America.

and clothing. On the frontier, women were frequently nurses and doctors for their families. Out of necessity, they learned to ride horses and use guns. Even upper-class women had plenty of work assuming responsibility for their households.

SERVANTS AND SLAVES

For the thousands of women who came to the Americas as indentured servants, life was immeasurably more difficult. These women, both white and black, were poor. In exchange for free passage to the colonies, they agreed to serve their employers on farms or in shops. Their service would last typically four to seven years without pay. Some indentured servant women were kidnapped and forced into service, but others chose the arrangement.

African-American women in slavery were in an even worse situation. Enslaved for life, they had no hope for freedom or equal rights. Their husbands and children were frequently sold away from them. Many became victims of sexual abuse and rape by the slave owners, and they had no right to defend themselves.

Slaves were not entitled to an education. Those who supported slavery claimed African Americans were of low intelligence and could not learn. One woman who disproved that lie was Phillis Wheatley, who was held as a slave in Boston, Massachusetts. Her owners taught her to

Phillis Wheatley's gift for poetry disproved many
misconceptions about African-American women.

read and write. They recognized she had a gift for poetry.
In 1776, a poem she wrote in praise of George Washington
was published in a magazine. Wheatley was invited to
meet Washington, and he congratulated her for her work.

NATIVE AMERICAN WOMEN'S RIGHTS

While European settlers considered women inferior, some Native American cultures held women in higher regard. The Iroquois, living in what is now the northeastern United States, were a matrilineal society, in which property and family lines passed down through women. If a couple separated, the mother would keep the children. The chiefs were male, but they were appointed by an elder woman in the clan. A council of female elders could remove a chief at any time. When Stanton and others began working for women's rights in the mid-1800s, they looked to the Iroquois as a model of a society where women held power.

The Cherokee people of the Southeast and Midwest were another matrilineal society. Women owned homes and fields, which passed down through their lines. Among the Pueblo people of Taos, New Mexico, the women built the houses, and female elders were respected. Women of the Plains nations also built the tepees, or homes, for their communities.

"REMEMBER THE LADIES"

In 1776, American leaders prepared to declare independence from Britain. The discussions of freedom and equality inspired women. Abigail Adams wrote a letter to her husband, John, who was a member of the

Continental Congress creating the laws that would govern the new nation. Abigail urged her husband to "remember the ladies":

> *In the new Code of Laws which I suppose it will be necessary for you to make I desire you would Remember the Ladies, & be more generous & favourable to them than your ancestors. Do not put such unlimited power into the hands of the Husbands. Remember all Men would be tyrants if they could. If particular care & attention is not paid to the [ladies], we are determined to [incite] a [rebellion], and will not*

FEMALE HEROES OF THE REVOLUTIONARY WAR

The American Revolution (1775–1783) saw its share of heroes. Paul Revere is well known for alerting Boston patriots about a British invasion in 1775. But when the British army attacked Danbury, Connecticut, in 1777, 16-year-old Sybil Ludington raised the alarm. She traveled 40 miles (64 km) by horseback in the middle of the night to raise a militia. For her heroic role, she was recognized by General George Washington.

Many colonial women took an active role against the British during the war. They organized boycotts, acted as spies and messengers, and aided on the battlefield. Women carried water to cool the cannons. One such woman, Mary Hays, became famous when she took her injured husband's place at the cannon and continued loading and firing. She was nicknamed Molly Pitcher. Other women, such as Deborah Sampson, dressed as men and picked up guns to fight.

hold ourselves bound by any Laws in which
we have no voice, or Representation.[3]

But John did not heed his wife's advice. He brushed off her ideas in a joking reply. "As to your extraordinary Code of Laws," he wrote, "I cannot but laugh."[4]

After the United States gained independence, John Adams went on to become the first vice president and the second president. His and other founding fathers' views about women's rights were reflected in the new country's laws. Women did not gain more freedom when the United States became a nation. Instead, they were granted even fewer rights. In colonial times, unmarried female property owners had been allowed to vote in elections. A woman was also allowed to vote on behalf of her family when the man of the house was unable. But in the years following independence, even these rights were taken away. Women lost all rights to vote in every state.

A CALL FOR EDUCATION

In colonial times, lower-class girls frequently received no education beyond what they could learn at home. Some upper-class girls attended elementary schools called dame schools. The girls learned reading, spelling, religion, and some basic arithmetic. They also learned sewing and embroidery. Women taught at dame schools. Boys attended master schools, taught by men. Boys learned higher mathematics, Latin, and Greek. Girls could attend master schools only when there was room, such as during the summer when the boys were working. However, this was not encouraged. As late as the 1870s, doctors claimed too much education could ruin a girl's health, possibly leading to a nervous breakdown or sterility.

In 1792, a groundbreaking book, *A Vindication of the Rights of Women* by Mary Wollstonecraft, was published in Britain. Wollstonecraft argued that women were not less intelligent than men as some experts claimed; they were just less educated. If women were to reach their full potential as human beings, they needed greater access to education.

A GIRLS' SCHOOL UNDER ATTACK

Prudence Crandall, a Quaker schoolteacher, believed African-American girls were entitled to an education. In 1833, she opened a school for African-American girls near Hartford, Connecticut, with approximately 20 students.[5] This was in the North, where few people supported slavery. Still, the community was strongly against Crandall's school. The windows were broken and the students had stones thrown at them. Masked townspeople tried burning down the building in the middle of the night. When that failed, they smashed in the walls. Fearing for her students' lives, Crandall was forced to close her school.

Oberlin College in Ohio was the first university to offer men and women access to higher education together.

Many American women shared this idea. In 1821, Emma Willard opened the Troy Female Seminary in Troy, New York. It was the first high school for girls. Her school taught young women subjects such as history, mathematics, and anatomy. Stanton was one of her students. In 1833, Oberlin College in Ohio became the first US college to become coeducational, accepting women as well as men. In the 1850s, Catharine Beecher opened the first "normal school," or teachers' college, to train women to become teachers.

By 1870, one-fifth of college and university students were women. And by 1900, that amount had increased to more than one-third.[6] More and more women were finding that education was the way forward.

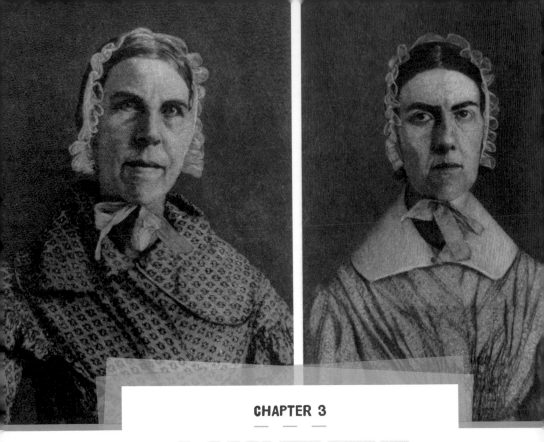

CHAPTER 3

A MOVEMENT EMERGES

T he 1800s were a time of change in the United States, later known as the reform era. Women began taking part in social reform movements. In particular, they fought for the abolition of slavery and the temperance movement, which was aimed at reducing or outlawing the sale of alcohol.

As they worked for change in society, women learned how to organize and fight for a cause. Barred from leadership positions in organizations with men, they often created their own organizations without men's involvement. And they gained the confidence to speak in public, even when people said it was improper. These valuable lessons would help them in their own fight for women's rights.

FEMALE ABOLITIONISTS SPEAK OUT

Women, both black and white, raised their voices and their pens against slavery. In the 1830s, women formed antislavery societies in various cities in the North, including

WOMEN AND THE TEMPERANCE MOVEMENT

Alcoholism was a serious problem in the 1800s. Members of the temperance movement urged people not to drink. They pushed to make alcohol sales illegal. In the early 1900s, activist Carrie Nation regularly entered saloons with a hatchet, smashing bottles and casks.

Many women joined the temperance movement. Some activists closely identified the cause with women's rights. When some men drank too much, their wives and children were left without money for food. Some wives were trapped with abusive, alcoholic husbands, unable to seek divorce without losing their children.

The temperance movement led to the passing of the Eighteenth Amendment, also known as Prohibition. It outlawed the manufacture and sale of alcohol in the United States in 1920. However, Prohibition failed to end drinking, as people continued producing and selling alcohol illegally. The amendment was repealed in 1933.

FROM CORSETS AND PETTICOATS TO BLOOMERS

In the 1800s, women wore long skirts with layers of petticoat skirts underneath, restricting their movement. They also wore corsets to make their waists appear small. These corsets were often so tight women had trouble breathing. It was nearly impossible for them to play sports or exercise vigorously. It only added to the belief that women were weak and delicate.

In 1851, Elizabeth Smith Miller came up with a daring new clothing alternative. She sewed herself a pair of pants, to be worn under a skirt. Her cousin Elizabeth Cady Stanton and their friend Amelia Bloomer loved the pants. Bloomer wrote about the pants in her newspaper, *The Lily.* The newspaper coverage sparked a fashion trend named after her. But the bloomer trend fizzled when women were teased, mocked, and even physically attacked in public for daring to wear so-called men's clothing. It was not until the 1890s, when the bicycle became popular, that it became acceptable for women to wear bloomers as sports clothing.

Philadelphia and Boston. Members organized fundraising events to support freed slaves. They also gathered thousands of signatures of women who opposed slavery and presented the petitions to the government. Since women could not vote, the petitions were their only political voice.

Two of the most controversial female abolitionists were sisters Sarah and Angelina Grimké. Raised on a plantation in South Carolina, they saw firsthand the horrors of slavery. As adults, they moved to Philadelphia, where they gave eloquent speeches informing people in the North about slavery.

The Grimkés were harshly criticized for speaking in public before a mixed audience of men and women. In 1837, a group of ministers wrote: "When [a woman] assumes the place and tone of a man as a public reformer . . . her character becomes unnatural." Sarah responded, "Whatsoever it is morally right for a man to do, it is morally right for a woman to do."[1] In February 1838, Angelina gave a speech against slavery in front of the Massachusetts legislature. She was the first woman ever to speak to a group of lawmakers in the United States.

On May 17, 1838, an anti-abolitionist mob in Philadelphia attacked and destroyed Pennsylvania Hall during the Anti-Slavery Convention for American Women. The convention featured speakers such as Angelina Grimké, Lucretia Mott, and Abby Kelley Foster. But even

WOMEN AGAINST SLAVERY

Harriet Tubman is perhaps the best-known female abolitionist. A former slave herself, she escaped from slavery in 1849 and led many more slaves to freedom through the Underground Railroad. In her later years, Tubman also spoke out in favor of women's rights, such as the right to vote. Tubman is known today as an American icon.

Harriet Beecher Stowe was another famous abolitionist. Her best-selling book *Uncle Tom's Cabin*, published in 1852, helped expose the evils of slavery.

the threat of death could not silence these brave women. They continued speaking despite the mob outside.

NOT TO BE PUSHED ASIDE

In June 1840, the World's Anti-Slavery Convention was held in London. Stanton attended with her husband, Henry, who was a delegate to the convention. Several female delegates had been invited, including Mott. But to the women's shock and outrage, the men decided the female delegates would not be allowed to vote or even speak—not even at a convention supporting justice and equality. The women were forced to act only as observers.

Mott and Stanton left the hall arm in arm, resolving to form a new society—one advocating the rights of women. Eight years later, they organized the historic women's rights convention in Seneca Falls. This was followed by many more regional gatherings.

JOINING FORCES

All over the country, powerful voices were coming together for the women's movement. Among them was leading abolitionist Lucy Stone, known for her bell-like voice. Antoinette Brown became the United States' first female ordained minister. Beginning in 1850, Stone and Brown, along with Paulina Wright Davis and others, organized an annual National Women's Rights Convention. Former slave

Sojourner Truth challenged those within the movement to recognize African-American women as an important part of the cause.

and abolitionist Sojourner Truth was one of the speakers at the convention at Worcester, Massachusetts, in 1850. Already well known for her antislavery speeches, Truth would become one of the most eloquent voices for women's

VOICES OF THE MOVEMENT

At a women's convention in Akron, Ohio, in 1851, abolitionist and former slave Sojourner Truth delivered what one listener called a "magical" speech.[2] After listening to men argue about why women deserved special, delicate treatment, she rose to her feet and asked to be heard:

"Look at me! Look at my arm! I have ploughed and planted, and gathered into barns, and no man could [do better than] me! And ain't I a woman? I could work as much and eat as much as a man—when I could get it—and bear the lash as well! And ain't I a woman? I have borne thirteen children, and seen most all sold off to slavery, and when I cried out with my mother's grief, none but Jesus heard me! And ain't I a woman?"[3]

rights. In 1851, she delivered her most famous speech, "Ain't I a Woman?" at a women's rights convention in Akron, Ohio.

Another woman who joined the women's rights cause and made it her life's work was Susan B. Anthony. Similar to Mott, Anthony had been raised a Quaker in a family that valued women and worked for reform. Anthony worked for the temperance movement.

In 1851, Stanton and Anthony met. They liked each other immediately and formed a lifelong partnership. Stanton and Anthony worked together to reform the marriage laws in the state of New York. Stanton had already helped lobby for the Married Women's Property Act of 1848, which allowed women in New York to inherit property. Working together, Anthony and

A POWERFUL PARTNERSHIP

Anthony and Stanton were quite different, but they made ideal partners in their work for women's rights. Stanton was a talented writer, while Anthony was a brilliant and tireless organizer. Anthony was often stern, while Stanton was fun loving and high-spirited. As the mother of seven children, Stanton was busy at home. But Anthony, who was single and childless, was free to travel from town to town, circulating petitions and holding meetings on women's rights. Soon the women developed a system: Stanton wrote the speeches, and Anthony delivered them. "I forged the thunderbolts; she fired them," Stanton explained.[4] Sometimes Anthony even helped with household duties and cared for Stanton's children so Stanton could write.

Stanton convinced the state legislature to strengthen that law. Their efforts led to the Married Women's Property Act of 1860, which allowed married women to maintain their property separate from their husbands' and keep their own earnings. Similar legislation also passed in other states.

WOMEN AT WORK

While women such as Anthony and Stanton worked toward change, others were busy working for a living. Industrial changes in the early 1800s sent some women to work in factories and mills. For the first time, they, too, earned a wage, although it was sometimes as low as half the pay men earned. By 1850, women made up nearly one-fourth of the paid workforce.[5]

"MILL GIRLS" ON STRIKE

In 1834 and 1836, female workers at a textile mill in Lowell, Massachusetts, went on strike to protest wage cuts, long hours, and poor working conditions. The mill owners fired the strike organizers. In response, hundreds of women walked off the job for days. Mill owners failed to meet their demands, but the women did not give up. In 1844, they formed a union, the Lowell Female Labor Reform Association. The first labor union for working women, it became a leading voice for workers in Lowell and other mill towns.

Close friends Stanton, *left*, and Anthony, *right*, inspired »
each other as much as they inspired the movement.

In the 1860s, more and more women were working as schoolteachers. But they received far less pay than men doing the same job.

It was still rare for women to enter professions other than teaching, but some women sought to change that. In 1849, Elizabeth Blackwell graduated from New York's Geneva Medical College. She was the first American woman to graduate from medical school and become a doctor. No hospital would hire her, so she started her own—the New York Infirmary for Women and Children. It was staffed entirely by women. In 1847, astronomer Maria Mitchell discovered a new comet. She became the only female member of the American Association for the Advancement of Science. These women were the first, the pioneers, in their fields.

Other women were pioneering new ideas about their roles in society. Between 1839 and 1844, American journalist and critic Margaret Fuller led conversations with other women in Boston about topics such as equality. She published *Women in the Nineteenth Century* in 1845, a groundbreaking feminist work. Her ideas would inspire women such as Elizabeth Cady Stanton to seek change in the decades to come. ⬤

Working in factories such as the Lowell Mill in »
Massachusetts was difficult, dirty, and dangerous, and
women were paid less than men for doing the same job.

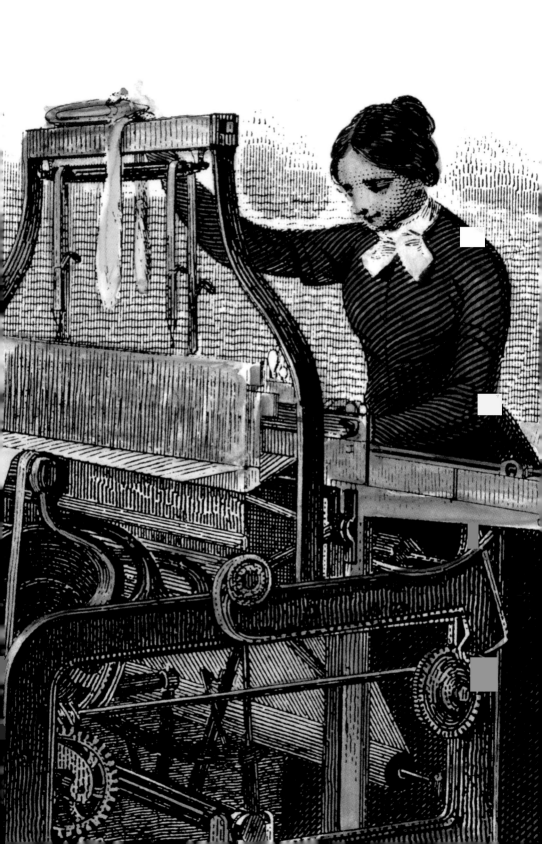

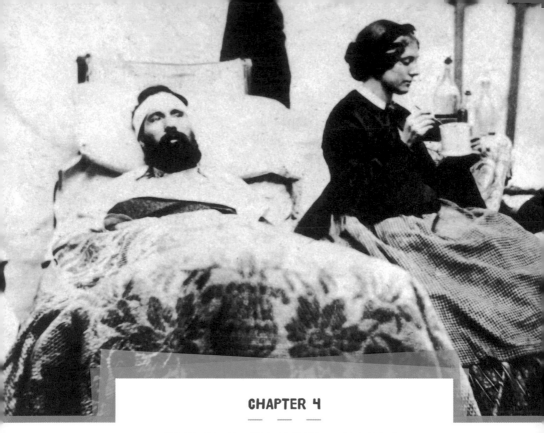

CHAPTER 4

FIGHTING FOR EQUALITY FOR ALL

n 1860, the national conflict over slavery erupted into the American Civil War (1861–1865). Women supported the Union as well as the Confederacy. Thousands worked as nurses, including Dorothea Dix and Clara Barton. Mary Walker became the first female army surgeon and the only woman yet to win the Congressional Medal of Honor for valor in battle. Other women served as scouts and spies. Back home, women ran their family farms and businesses. They did "men's work" while the men were away fighting.

In January 1865, the Thirteenth Amendment passed, abolishing slavery. Three months later, the Civil War was over. Women's wartime efforts had gained them more public respect than ever before. President Abraham Lincoln praised the women, saying, "If all that has been said by orators and poets since the creation of the world were applied to the women of America, it would not do them justice for their conduct during this war."[1]

With the war over and slavery abolished, women hoped for a new era of equality for all Americans. But sadly,

ANGELS OF THE BATTLEFIELD

Barton came to be known as the "Angel of the Battlefield" for her courageous actions as a nurse during the American Civil War. Barton risked her life to bring supplies and support to soldiers on the front lines. In 1881, she went on to form the American Red Cross. The organization provides emergency assistance and disaster relief in the United States.

Dix was another famous nurse. As superintendent of nurses for the Union Army of the North, she insisted on giving first aid to the wounded Confederate soldiers as well as to the Union soldiers. Dix also created the first hospitals in the United States for people with mental illness.

BLACK WOMEN UNITE FOR RIGHTS

African-American women faced double discrimination for both their sex and their race after the Civil War. They were pushed into the lowest-paying jobs in the country. African-American women felt cut off from the mainstream women's rights movement, which tended to represent the white middle class. In Southern states, African-American women were banned from joining white women's suffrage groups. So, all over the country, black women formed their own clubs. In 1896, black women activists including Harriet Tubman, writer Frances Harper, and organizer Mary Church Terrell founded the National Association of Colored Women. The organization brought together more than 100 black women's clubs working for women's suffrage and other civil and political rights.

they found they were still far from their goal of equal rights.

AMENDING THE CONSTITUTION

With the passage of the Thirteenth Amendment, women who had worked for abolition were proud. They had helped the slaves win their freedom. But much more work had to be done. New laws were needed to guarantee former slaves their full rights as citizens. Stanton and Anthony helped form the American Equal Rights Association, an organization dedicated to gaining voting rights for all citizens, including African Americans and women. "No country ever has had or ever will have peace until every citizen has a voice in the government," Stanton declared. "Now, let us try universal suffrage."[2]

But again, male lawmakers pushed women's rights aside. They claimed African-American men needed the vote first. "One question at a time," argued abolitionist Wendell Phillips.[3] Women would have to wait. The Fourteenth Amendment was ratified in 1868, guaranteeing voting rights for all male citizens. This meant African-American men could vote, but women of any race could not. Anthony, Stanton, and others fought to have the word *male* taken out, but to no avail. The amendment's supporters feared it would not pass if women were included.

Next, the Fifteenth Amendment was ratified in 1870 to strengthen African Americans' right to vote. It guaranteed that all citizens, regardless of their "race, color, or previous condition of servitude," could vote.[4] Nothing was said about sex. Women still could not vote.

RIVAL ORGANIZATIONS

In 1869, women's rights activists formed two new organizations. One was the National Woman Suffrage Association (NWSA), created by Stanton and Anthony. In 1876, the NWSA issued a "Declaration of Rights of the Women of the United States" on the one-hundredth anniversary of the US Declaration of Independence. Their declaration stated,

> We ask justice, we ask equality, we ask that
> all civil and political rights that belong to the
> citizens of the United States be guaranteed
> to us and our daughters forever.[5]

The other new organization formed around the same time was the American Woman Suffrage Association (AWSA), led by Lucy Stone and her husband, Henry Blackwell, along with Julia Ward Howe. The two rival organizations both fought for women's suffrage, but they did not agree on how it should be achieved.

The AWSA was more conservative. It had supported the Fourteenth and Fifteenth Amendments and now sought to win women's suffrage gradually state by state. The NWSA was more radical. Its leaders had rejected the amendments and continued to demand women's suffrage through a change to the Constitution.

LUCY STONERS

When she married Henry Blackwell in 1855, Lucy Stone chose not to take his name, as a sign that she was not changing who she was in order to marry. This was an unusual choice, unheard of at the time. Other feminists, such as Elizabeth Cady Stanton, kept their maiden names but used them as middle names. Women who followed Stone's example were called "Lucy Stoners."

Similar to Anthony, many women across the country attempted voting in order to test the new laws.

SUSAN B. ANTHONY GOES TO JAIL

"Well I have been & gone & done it!!"[6] exclaimed Anthony in a letter to Stanton dated November 5, 1872. She had cast a vote in the presidential election. Anthony was not alone. Fifteen other women from her election ward had followed suit.[7] In total, approximately 150 women had attempted to vote in the 1872 election.[8] Their goal was to be arrested. Then they would challenge the new amendments in court.

Most of the women had been turned away at the polls. But a few, such as Anthony, succeeded in voting. For her daring act, Anthony was arrested, jailed, and fined. She refused to pay, declaring that voting was her right as a citizen. "In your ordered verdict of guilty," she told the judge, "you have trampled under foot every vital principle of our government. My natural rights, my civil rights, my political rights, my judicial rights are all alike ignored."[9] Although she lost her case, Anthony's arrest made headlines and gained publicity for the cause.

Virginia Minor also attempted to vote and was refused at the polls. She ultimately took her case to the Supreme Court in 1875. She, too, argued that since women were citizens, they had every right to vote. But the Supreme Court disagreed. In *Minor v. Happersett*, the court ruled that the concept of

WOMEN'S RIGHTS NEWSPAPERS

In the late 1800s, women's rights activists used newspapers to spread their message. *The Revolution*, founded in 1868 by the NWSA, had the motto, "Men, their rights and nothing more; women, their rights and nothing less!"[10] A rival newspaper was the *Women's Journal*, founded by the AWSA in 1870.

citizenship meant "membership in a nation and nothing more."[11] Citizenship did not guarantee voting rights, the court claimed. It was up to each state to decide who could vote. This decision had devastating consequences nationwide for women as well as some men. States in the South passed new laws designed to stop African Americans from voting, too, by requiring them to take literacy tests or own property.

COMBINING FORCES

Women's rights activists now realized it would be quite difficult to win the vote through the courts. The laws were clearly against women. To get the vote, women would have to change the laws state by state—while also continue trying to amend the flawed national Constitution.

Anthony and Stanton drafted a proposed women's suffrage amendment in January 1878. When they presented the proposal to Congress, lawmakers did not even pretend to be interested. They did not bother to vote on it that year. Year after year, as the amendment was presented to Congress, it was rejected. The so-called Susan B. Anthony Amendment would have to be reintroduced nearly every year for 42 years.

In 1890, the rival NWSA and AWSA organizations combined to form a new group, the National American Woman Suffrage Association (NAWSA). Stanton became

the organization's first president, followed by Anthony. In 1900, Anthony retired. Led next by Carrie Chapman Catt, the NAWSA continued working with other groups to organize peaceful protests across the nation. The stage was set for the new century. ●

« Carrie Chapman Catt became the president of the newly formed National American Woman Suffrage Association.

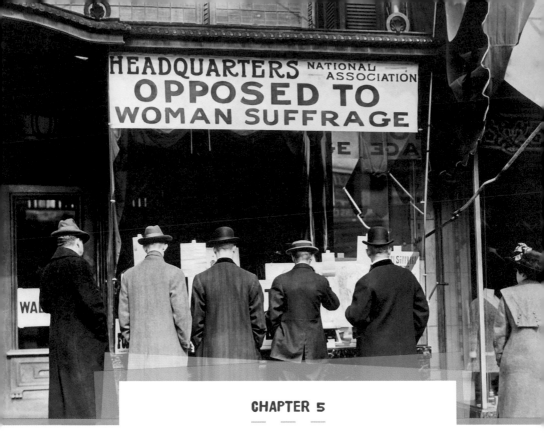

CHAPTER 5

GETTING
THE VOTE

T
he 1800s came to a close. Well into the 1900s, women's suffrage was still highly controversial. Women suffragists, also called suffragettes, were ridiculed in the press. Newspaper cartoonists depicted them as bitter and unattractive old maids or as neglectful wives, eager to leave their crying babies with hapless husbands while they went off to the polls.

Women's suffrage was unpopular for many reasons. Some feared it would destroy families as women became more interested in politics than in caring for their homes. Others feared that if women gained full equality to men, they could lose special privileges and be drafted into war.

Even many women outside the movement lacked interest in or opposed the cause. Some women claimed they did not need to vote. They thought their vote would not matter if they voted the same way their husbands did. Some upper-class women feared they would lose their special political influence if all women could vote. In other

WORKING WOMEN'S RIGHTS

As upper-class women fought for the vote, some working-class women were fighting for their labor rights as well. The Women's Trade Union League, formed in 1903, supported women's strikes in factories. By 1917, 41 states had laws protecting women workers. The laws limited the number of work hours and the amount of weight they could lift on the job.

Reform also came after disasters occurred, notably the 1911 fire at the Triangle Shirtwaist factory in New York City. Some 146 workers, nearly all young immigrant women, died in the fire because the factory owners kept exits locked to prevent workers from stealing or taking breaks. Outrage over the tragedy led to stricter safety laws for factories and other workplaces. The International Ladies' Garment Workers' Union led the charge, growing to become one of the largest and most influential unions in America.

cases, many women likely supported the right but refused to do so publicly. Women's social class also had an impact. Most lower-class women were so busy working day to day they did not have time to take action for their rights. But nonetheless, the movement was growing.

WOMEN'S REPRODUCTIVE RIGHTS

While suffragists were fighting for women's voting rights, Margaret Sanger was fighting for their reproductive rights. As a nurse, Sanger saw women living in poverty with children they struggled to support. One patient, Sadie, begged for advice. She was desperate to prevent more pregnancies, but Sanger could not help. It was illegal to dispense birth control or even provide information about it.

In 1914, Sanger began teaching about birth control. She was arrested and put in jail. Undeterred, she started her own clinic in 1916. Some 100 women lined up at the door the day it opened.[1] Again, she was arrested. But her appeal in court led to a change in laws. She was able to reopen her clinic in 1921. The organization she founded later became known as Planned Parenthood. "No woman," Sanger said, "can call herself free unless she can decide for herself whether and when to become a mother."[2]

STANTON'S AND ANTHONY'S LAST YEARS

Advancing in age, Anthony and Stanton realized they would not live to see their goal realized. Congress was still dismissing their amendment every year. But they continued speaking about suffrage and other women's rights issues in hopes that life would be better for the next generation of women. "We are sowing winter wheat," Stanton confessed in her diary, "which the coming spring will see sprout and which other hands than ours will reap and enjoy."[3] She died in 1902 at age 86.

Anthony, known affectionately as "Aunt Susan" to a new generation of young women activists, continued organizing conferences and conducting speaking tours well into her 80s. She died in 1906 at age 86. In her last public speech, she concluded with optimism about the future of the movement, saying, "Failure is impossible!"[4]

STATE BY STATE

Although the suffrage amendment was stalled at the national level, the suffrage movement gradually made progress state by state, especially in the West. There were fewer women living in those states, and attitudes about women were less traditional. When it entered the Union in 1890, Wyoming became the first state to grant women full voting rights. From 1893 to 1912, eight more Western states granted suffrage to women.

Other states followed, due to the hard work of women's groups who gathered petitions and changed minds. On March 3, 1913, more than 5,000 women marched in a parade in Washington, DC, in support of suffrage.[5] The parade, organized by suffragist Alice Paul, was such a success that US Army troops had to control the

In 1913, thousands of women marched in New York and other cities across the country to show support for suffrage.

crowds. The newly elected president, Woodrow Wilson, was just arriving in Washington for his inauguration the next day, and he wondered why no crowds greeted him. "They're off watching the women," he was told.[6]

From 1913 to 1918, the next wave of states adopted women's suffrage laws. In Illinois, journalist Ida B. Wells-Barnett founded the first black women's suffrage group, the Alpha Suffrage Club of Chicago.

THE NIGHT OF TERROR

While the NAWSA continued lobbying for legislative change by means of petitions and letters, the National Women's Party (NWP) used bolder tactics. Led by Paul, the fiery organizer from New Jersey, NWP members began picketing the White House. They carried signs that asked for the vote. Although this form of protest was legal, some picketers were arrested. Paul, journalist Dorothy Day, and others went on a hunger strike in jail to protest their unfair arrest. They were force-fed by angry prison guards. On November 15,

IDA B. WELLS-BARNETT

Wells-Barnett was a champion of equal rights for African Americans and women. As editor and cofounder of the *Memphis Free Speech and Headlight*, she wrote many articles exposing the horrors of racially motivated crimes, especially lynchings. Wells-Barnett worked alongside Anthony and other leaders in the fight for women's rights. She founded the first black women's suffrage group, the Alpha Suffrage Club of Chicago, in 1913. The club's efforts would later help Illinois become the first state to approve the Susan B. Anthony Amendment in 1919.

At a women's suffrage parade in Washington, DC, in 1913, event leaders told Wells-Barnett she could not march with the white women from Chicago. They said she had to join the other African-American women at the rear. Refusing to remain segregated from her fellow Chicagoans, Wells-Barnett waited until the parade had started, then slipped into step alongside the white women.

1917, the hostility culminated in what was called the Night of Terror, when 33 suffragists were beaten by prison guards.

When the incident became public, people were outraged. They pressured President Wilson and Congress to back the suffrage amendment first drafted by Stanton and Anthony in 1878. It finally passed the House of Representatives on January 10, 1918, and was ratified by the Senate in 1919 as the Nineteenth Amendment.

But 36 states had to ratify the amendment before it could officially be added to the Constitution. One by one, the states agreed. The last, Tennessee, voted to ratify the amendment on August 18, 1920. "To get the word 'male' in effect out of the Constitution cost the women of the country fifty-two years of pauseless campaign," noted NAWSA president Catt.[7]

TERROR AT THE WHITE HOUSE

On November 15, 1917, 33 women stood outside the White House, holding signs asking President Woodrow Wilson for the right to vote. Police arrested the picketers for "obstructing sidewalk traffic" and took them to jail.[8] There, the terror began. Guards took out their clubs. They beat, kicked, and slammed the women against walls. One woman, Lucy Burns, was left hanging by chains from her cell all night. Another was knocked unconscious. Public outrage over the incident pressured President Wilson to support the Susan B. Anthony Amendment.

Noted suffragists Carrie Catt, *left*, and Mary Garrett Hay, *right*, cast well-earned votes on Election Day 1920.

A PROMISE FULFILLED

On November 2, 1920, more than 8 million women across every precinct in the United States went to the polls to exercise their right to vote.[9] In the Declaration of Independence, Thomas Jefferson had proclaimed equality for all, but it had taken 144 years for women to be included in that promise. Only one of the women who signed the Declaration of Sentiments in 1848 was still alive to see the day women got to vote. Charlotte Woodward Pierce was 91 years old. ●

CHAPTER 6

WOMEN'S CHANGING IMAGE

Now that they had won the vote, women were also running for office. In 1917, Jeannette Rankin became the first woman elected to the US Congress, representing the state of Montana. "We're half the people; we should be half the Congress," Rankin said.[1] In 1925, Nellie Tayloe Ross became governor of Wyoming. In 1932, Hattie Caraway was elected to the US Senate from

Arkansas. Frances Perkins became the first woman to serve in a presidential cabinet. In 1933, President Franklin Roosevelt appointed her secretary of labor.

After securing the right to vote, the NAWSA changed its name to the League of Women Voters (LWV) and focused on helping women become informed citizens. The smaller, more radical NWP pushed ahead for more change. In 1923, they introduced a proposed Equal Rights Amendment, or ERA. The amendment declared, "Men and women shall have equal rights throughout the United States."[2] However, the LWV and other labor supporters rejected the ERA. They worried that declaring women equal to men could actually be bad for working women. It would mean giving up some of the laws that had been created to protect women in the workplace.

THE NEW WOMAN

Since the beginning of the women's rights movement, the image of American women had been changing. The "New Woman" of the late 1800s and early 1900s put aside hoopskirts, corsets, and other restrictive clothing styles. Women rode bicycles, played basketball, went to college, and demanded the right to vote. During the 1920s, often known as the Roaring Twenties, the flapper look came into fashion. Young women chopped their long hair into

FUNCTIONAL FASHION

Beginning in the 1890s, women began dancing, exercising, riding bicycles, and playing organized sports such as basketball. With this new activity, women gave up corsets and long skirts in favor of the bloomers first created in 1851. Doctors still mistakenly warned that women should not overexert themselves in sport and dance. They claimed such exertion might ruin their health.

By the 1920s, women were wearing one-piece bathing suits that showed bare arms and legs. By today's standards, these suits look modest. However, they were shocking at the time. Women could be arrested on the beach for showing too much skin.

short bobs. They wore makeup, which was previously thought to be only for girls with poor reputations. And they shunned long skirts in favor of short, loose, shapeless dresses that made them look more boyish than womanly.

Flappers drew criticism for so-called immoral behavior, such as smoking, drinking, and doing wild new dances such as the Charleston. But in doing so, these women challenged what society thought women could do. For the next several decades, women's roles continued changing.

WOMEN IN THE GREAT DEPRESSION

As the nation sunk into the Great Depression of the 1930s, women's rights hit a roadblock that would last several decades. The Great Depression began with a massive stock market crash in 1929 and lasted through 1942. It weakened women's standards of living as well as men's. Jobs were scarce, and many employers refused to hire women. Employers believed the few jobs available should be spared for men, the traditional family providers. Women who did find work were forced into lower-paying jobs.

But women such as Secretary of Labor Perkins were involved in crafting President Roosevelt's New Deal, a program that brought aid to families and helped get the country back on its feet. President Roosevelt appointed an African-American woman, educator and civil rights leader Mary McLeod Bethune, to head the Office of Minority Affairs.

First Lady Eleanor Roosevelt also became a women's rights icon. She took a more visible political role than any First Lady had in the past. She published a daily newspaper column and held weekly press conferences with female reporters. She worked with her husband to prioritize issues on her agenda: peace, education, aid to the needy, and better treatment for women and minorities.

WOMEN IN WORLD WAR II

Women had always played active roles during US wars, dating back to the American Revolution. Those roles were

A real-life "Rosie the Riveter" helps assemble a bomber plane during World War II.

expanded even more in World War II (1939–1945). Women were invited to serve in the branches of the armed forces, in the Women's Army Corps (WAC), the nursing corps, and the reserves for the US Navy, Coast Guard, and Marines.

On the home front, 6 million women joined the workforce, taking jobs vacated by men going off to war.[3] For the first time, women were actively recruited for jobs traditionally held by men, such as welding, riveting, cutting laths, and running drills in war plants. Minority women, too, found jobs for which they never would have been considered before.

POSTWAR WOMEN

After the end of World War II in 1945, the United States entered a period of prosperity. More middle-class Americans than ever before could afford cars and nice homes in the suburbs. Everything seemed to be in place for the "American Dream" to become a reality.

But the American Dream boxed women into a specific role. During the war years, women had assumed men's jobs. They learned they could do nearly anything a man could do. But when the war ended and the men returned to the factories, women were sent home to be wives and mothers. The median age for

ROSIE THE RIVETER

When American men were called to fight in World War I and World War II, women took their places in factories and businesses across the nation. A song called "Rosie the Riveter" was popular in 1942. It celebrated an imaginary woman working in a factory driving rivets, or fasteners, onto the hulls of B-19 bombers. The government and private companies recruited women for such wartime work through posters and other advertising. One such poster from the World War II era became famous when it was rediscovered by the women's movement. Titled "We Can Do It!" the poster portrays a woman with her hair tied into a red kerchief, rolling up her sleeves, and flexing her muscles. Back then and today, the image celebrates the power of women.

marriage for women was 20, and the nation went into a baby boom.[4] Magazines and television glorified the "happy homemaker," the perfect wife and mother who delighted in baking pies, waxing floors, and caring for her family. And yet the truth was that many women were unhappy with this limited role. They felt empty and useless, and they longed for something more.

Many women, married and unmarried, still worked. In fact, in 1950, 30 percent of the workforce was female.[5] But they were limited to lower-paying positions, such as secretaries, salesclerks, housekeepers, assembly-line workers, or waitresses. In 1963, their average wage was 59 percent of what men earned for similar work.[6]

Breaking into higher-paid work was nearly impossible. Even college-educated women were expected to be wives and mothers without careers of their own. Many people even assumed women only attended college to find husbands, not to pursue careers. Medical schools and law schools frequently refused to admit women. Once out of college, women found few job opportunities, and they were expected to quit when they got married. Those women who did attempt to enter a profession found themselves shut out from the "men's club," victims of sexual discrimination and even sexual harassment.

Author Betty Friedan opened the nation's eyes to this problem in her book *The Feminine Mystique*, published in

1963. In it, she explained the problem was that women were being limited in society. Forced into gender roles, Friedan claimed, women were prevented from becoming all they could be. "It was a strange stirring, a sense of dissatisfaction, a yearning that women suffered," she wrote.[7]

Friedan's *The Feminine Mystique* became an instant best seller and touched off what became known as the second wave of the women's rights movement. The first wave had begun more than 100 years earlier, at the Seneca Falls Convention in 1848. The full force of that wave had died out

"THIS FIRM HAS NEVER HIRED A WOMAN LAWYER"

Even women who managed to obtain professional degrees often had trouble securing jobs. In 1952, Sandra Day O'Connor graduated from Stanford Law School. She was among the top students of her class, but no law firm would hire her. When a friend's father gave her an interview as a favor, she recalled:

> He looked at my résumé: "Oh, you have a fine résumé, Ms. Day, fine. But Ms. Day, this firm has never hired a woman lawyer. . . . Our clients wouldn't stand for it." . . . And he said, "If you can type well enough, I might be able to get you on as a legal secretary." I said, "That isn't the job that I want to find."[8]

O'Connor eventually got her start by working for free for another attorney. Over time, she had a brilliant career. In 1981, she made history when she was appointed the first female justice to the US Supreme Court.

VOICES OF THE MOVEMENT

In Betty Friedan's groundbreaking feminist work, *The Feminine Mystique*, an anonymous housewife described the sense of unfulfillment so common to American women in postwar society:

"I've tried everything women are supposed to do . . . . I can do it all, and I like it, but it doesn't leave you anything to think about—any feeling of who you are. I never had any career ambitions. All I wanted was to get married and have four children. I love the kids and Bob and my home. There's no problem you can even put a name to. But I'm desperate. I begin to feel I have no personality. I'm a server of food and a putter-on of pants and a bedmaker, somebody who can be called on when you want something. But who am I?" [9]

Women in the **1950s** were expected to be happy homemakers, but this life left many of them unfulfilled.

after suffrage was achieved in 1920. Now the women's movement gathered momentum once again. Activists prepared to make another historic push for change.

CHAPTER 7

THE SECOND
WAVE

T he 1960s and 1970s were a time of social reform in the United States. Thousands marched for civil rights, demanding an end to racist laws discriminating against African Americans. Others demonstrated for peace, calling for the government to end the United States' involvement in the Vietnam War (1955–1975). The second wave of the women's rights movement, also known as the feminist movement or

women's liberation, was
an important part of
the times.

LAWS FOR
WOMEN IN THE
WORKPLACE

During the 1960s and
1970s, women pressured
the government to take
action to protect their
rights. President John
F. Kennedy ordered a
Presidential Commission
on the Status of Women
in 1961. The commission
found that American
women faced widespread
inequalities, including
fewer opportunities for
education, unequal pay,
and lack of affordable
child care. In response,
Congress passed the
Equal Pay Act in 1963.

WOMEN IN OTHER
SOCIAL MOVEMENTS

The feminist movement was one
of many social movements women
were involved in. Women also
played significant roles in the
civil rights movement and the
antiwar movement.

In 1955, Rosa Parks refused
to sit at the back of a bus in
Montgomery, Alabama, as black
people were required to do at the
time. Her courageous act helped
spark the civil rights movement.
As the movement continued, other
black women, such as Fannie Lou
Hamer and Angela Davis, became
prominent leaders in the fight for
African-American equality.

In 1961, during the Cold War
between the United States and the
Soviet Union, some 50,000 women
gathered in 60 US cities to stage
a demonstration against nuclear
weapons. The protest, organized
by the group Women Strike for
Peace, was the largest women's
peace demonstration of the
century. Women Strike for Peace
was also active in protesting the
Vietnam War.

DOLORES HUERTA AND THE UNITED FARM WORKERS

While some women fought for equality in offices, others needed better working conditions in factories and farm fields. Dolores Huerta fought for them. With César Chávez, she cofounded the United Farm Workers in 1962, a union that helped migrant farm workers negotiate for better working conditions. Many of the workers were Asian and Latin American immigrants. Huerta helped organize boycotts of grapes and lettuce, products grown with migrant labor. Huerta was arrested many times and even beaten, but she continues to work today in support of migrants.

Its goal was to provide equal pay for men and women doing equivalent work. However, the act did not cover many types of employment. It did not cover domestics, agricultural workers, executives, administrators, or professionals. More legislation was needed.

In 1964, Congress was working to pass the Civil Rights Act intended to outlaw discrimination against African Americans. Possibly hoping to defeat the bill, Howard Smith, a Southern congressman, added something extra to it—words that outlawed discrimination on the basis of sex. The new wording was met with laughter in Congress. But the bill passed anyway. Title VII of the Civil Rights Act outlawed job discrimination on the basis of "race, color, religion, sex, or national origin."[1] A new federal agency was created to enforce this law: the Equal Employment Opportunity Commission (EEOC).

In its first year, the EEOC expected to receive not more than 2,000 complaints. It received more than 8,800, creating an immediate backlog of cases to be investigated.[2] But as more and more of these complaints were ignored or dismissed, it became obvious the EEOC was not doing its job.

EQUAL RIGHTS NOW!

In June 1966, Friedan sat down at a table in Washington, DC, with a group of women. They were angry about the EEOC and its failure to help women. Friedan wrote the word *NOW* on a paper napkin. This would be the name of a new organization: the National Organization for Women (NOW). Its purpose was "to take *action* to bring women into full participation in the mainstream of American society . . . in truly equal partnership with men."[3]

On August 26, 1970, NOW organized a nationwide Women's Strike for Equality. More than 50,000 people, both men and women, participated in a protest march in New York City alone.[4] Their goals were increased equality for women in jobs and education, as well as access to child care and birth control. Other women's groups joined the demonstrations, including the Young Women's Christian Association (YWCA) and the radical Redstockings.

Women unite to demonstrate during NOW's
Women's Strike for Equality in 1970.

The movement had expanded. Ordinary American women
who had never been politically active before were now
calling themselves feminists. "It exceeded my wildest
dreams," Friedan said. "It's now a political movement and
the message is clear."[5]

As the movement spread, the opposition argued that
feminist issues such as reproductive rights, child care,
and sharing of household duties were personal matters.
Opponents believed women needed to resolve these issues
within their own families, not in the political arena. But
activists stressed to both men and women that these
"personal" issues were actually signs of widespread

discrimination that needed to change on the political level. "The personal is political" became a popular slogan to help the public see the issues in a new light.[6]

WOMEN GAIN POLITICAL POWER

Some 50 years after women had gained the right to vote, they were still vastly underrepresented in government. In 1965, Asian American Patsy Matsu Takemoto Mink of Hawaii became the first minority woman elected to Congress. In 1968, Shirley Chisholm became the first African-American woman elected to Congress, as a representative from New York City. She later ran for president of the United States in 1972, becoming the first African American to do so. In 1970, Bella Abzug, also of New York, was elected to Congress with the slogan, "This woman's place is in the House—the House of Representatives!"[7]

In 1971, Friedan, Abzug, Chisholm, journalist Gloria Steinem, and other leading feminists established the National Women's Political Caucus (NWPC). Their goal was to recruit and train feminist-minded women for government positions and help them get elected. They also lobbied for prowoman causes such as better education and a ban on discrimination. At the founding of the caucus, Steinem stated, "This is no simple reform. It really is a revolution."[8]

EQUAL EMPLOYMENT OPPORTUNITY ACT AND TITLE IX

The Equal Pay Act and the Civil Rights Act were beginning to make a difference in women's lives. But they did not address all types of discrimination women faced. The NWPC and other women's groups continued lobbying for more laws to address discrimination in schools and the workplace.

Job discrimination was a big problem. Until the 1970s, there were typically two job sections in a newspaper: one listing jobs for men and another listing jobs for women. Employers could even specify the age, race, or marital status of the people they wanted to hire. For example, many employers openly preferred young, white,

GLORIA STEINEM

In 1963, journalist Gloria Steinem became famous for her "I Was a Playboy Bunny" exposé. Her article described what it was like to work as a waitress in New York City's Playboy Club, a nightclub operated by the corporation behind *Playboy* magazine. Steinem worked undercover for three weeks as a Playboy Bunny waitress. She wore a revealing corset, high heels, and a bunny tail and ears. The job had been advertised as fun and glamorous. But instead, Steinem found it uncomfortable and humiliating. Her report shined a spotlight on the low wages, long hours, sexual harassment, and degrading conditions women faced at the Playboy Club and in many other serving jobs.

In the 1970s, Steinem would help launch the NWPC and start *Ms.*, a feminist magazine. She became a prominent leader in the feminist movement.

single women for service jobs such as receptionists, food servers, or flight attendants. Flight attendants could be fired after they married or when they reached the age of 32.[9] In 1972, President Richard Nixon issued the Equal Employment Opportunity Act to outlaw this type of job discrimination.

A similar problem was occurring in education. Because of sexism, many more men than women were admitted to colleges and universities. There were far more athletic programs for men than for women, and schools did not offer athletic scholarships for women. To reduce this type of discrimination in education, President Nixon signed a bill known as Title IX in 1972. It bans sex discrimination in educational institutions that receive funding from the government, including public schools and universities. Over the next decades, the law would have remarkable results, leading to greatly increased numbers of women in sports and higher education.

ANOTHER PUSH FOR THE ERA

Suffragist Alice Paul had first introduced the Equal Rights Amendment (ERA) in 1923. It had failed year after year to win approval by Congress, until March 22, 1972. The ERA stated: "Equality of rights under the law shall not be denied or abridged by the United States or by any State on account of sex."[10] Feminists believed this amendment would ensure women's full equality in the eyes of the law.

But if the ERA were to become part of the Constitution, at least 38 states had to ratify it within eight years. NOW and other groups rallied to support the amendment across the country. Success looked hopeful at first. The ERA secured 22 state ratifications in the first year.[11]

WOMEN'S RIGHTS AND ABORTION

An important issue for the women's movement then and now is the right to choose when to have a family. Abortion was illegal in most states until 1973. Then in *Roe v. Wade*, the Supreme Court ruled that restricting abortion violated women's constitutional right to privacy. It was a landmark case in which the Supreme Court sided with feminists and others who argued that a woman has a right to control her own body. After the decision, abortion became legal in all 50 states. Although many feminists viewed this as a victory, the decision remains highly controversial today.

But the opposition—most famously Phyllis Schlafly—was determined to stop it. Although she claimed to be a simple housewife, Schlafly was a Harvard-educated lawyer and savvy political activist. In 1973, she founded an organization called STOP ERA. STOP was an acronym for Stop Taking Our Privileges. She warned the ERA would destroy family values and deprive women of protections they enjoyed,

Despite the efforts of, *from left*, Friedan, Abzug, and Steinem in the late 1970s, the ERA failed to win approval from enough states by 1982.

such as the right to be supported by a husband. Echoing critics of the suffrage movement during World War I, Schlafly also warned if the ERA were passed, women might be drafted into combat.

As the opposition gained strength, ratification slowed. By 1977, 35 out of the needed 38 states had ratified the ERA. But by 1982, the deadline for ratification, US politics had grown more conservative. Despite the efforts from feminist groups, the amendment did not receive approval from enough states to become law. The painful defeat signaled to some that the women's movement might be over.

CHAPTER 8

BACKLASH AND THE THIRD WAVE

The women's movement of the 1960s and 1970s brought tremendous changes. Women were demanding more power in the workplace and in their families. However, some people did not like the impact these changes had on society. As the years passed into the 1980s and 1990s, political conservatives led a backlash against feminists and the changes they had achieved.

For instance, some conservatives blamed the increasing divorce rate on the feminist movement. The divorce rate had gone up dramatically—from 10 percent in the 1960s to 50 percent in the 1990s.[1] This was partly because women had better employment opportunities and could support themselves after a divorce. Also, new no-fault divorce laws enacted in the 1960s and 1970s made it easier for women to end their marriages. Before the no-fault divorce laws, women seeking a divorce had to prove in court that their husbands had been abusive or unfaithful, which was not easy to do.

Conservatives did not necessarily reject all the advances of the women's movement. But many conservatives felt the movement had gone too far and had become too radical. Their criticisms caused a backlash against feminism in the 1980s and 1990s. In the subtitle of her 1991 book *Backlash*, Susan Faludi

GERALDINE FERRARO

Amidst the conservative backlash against feminists in the 1980s and early 1990s, a political inspiration emerged. In 1984, Geraldine Ferraro became the first woman to run for vice president. She was the running mate of Democratic presidential candidate Walter Mondale. Incumbent Ronald Reagan won the election by a landslide, but Ferraro's milestone remained an inspiration for women. "If we can do this," Ferraro said of her nomination, "we can do anything."[2]

described the problem as an "undeclared war against American women."[3]

Conservative religious leaders such as preacher Jerry Falwell were leading the negative attacks. Falwell labeled feminists as prodivorce, proabortion, and antifamily. He called for a "moral majority" of Americans to come together and support a return to what they saw as traditional morals and values.

During this time of the 1980s and early 1990s, Washington, DC, was dominated by conservatives. President Ronald Reagan served two terms, from 1981 to 1989. George H. W. Bush followed as president from 1989 to 1993.

WOMEN IN THE MILITARY

Despite the backlash that continued into the 1990s, women saw increased representation in the US military. For instance, women made up nearly 7 percent of active military in the Persian Gulf War of 1991.[4]

But a controversy in 1995 illustrated the barriers that still remained for women in the military. That year, Shannon Faulkner was accepted into the Citadel, an all-male military academy in South Carolina. Because both sexes use the name Shannon, Citadel officials assumed she was male. When the school learned she was female, they tried to revoke her admission. She fought them in court and won. Faulkner enrolled in the school but quit after only five days. Other cadets had harassed and threatened her. Her experience opened a door for other women, however. As of 2012, more than 300 female students had graduated from the school.[5]

These presidents supported this conservative agenda, which included opposing the ERA and outlawing abortion. It seemed to feminists that just as women had started to get ahead, some people in society wanted to push them back again.

THE ANITA HILL-CLARENCE THOMAS CONTROVERSY

In 1991, a controversy broke out that pitted feminists against conservatives in a dramatic way. President George H. W. Bush nominated Clarence Thomas to the Supreme Court. Thomas, a political conservative, was set to become the second African-American justice in history to sit on the nation's highest court. Then Anita Hill, his former subordinate, came forward to say Thomas had sexually harassed her.

Millions of Americans watched the Senate Judiciary Committee case unfold on television. Thomas denied the accusations and was ultimately appointed. Yet many Americans—not just feminists—believed Hill's accusations and were angry Thomas had been appointed. They questioned whether the all-white, all-male Senate committee had taken Hill, an African-American woman, seriously. Many saw the incident as a sign women needed more support in government.

SEXUAL HARASSMENT

Sexual harassment in the workplace is an unlawful form of sex discrimination and a violation of Title VII of the Civil Rights Act of 1964. In the 1970s, lawyer Catharine MacKinnon first legally established sexual harassment as a form of sex discrimination, which the US Supreme Court later upheld in 1986.

According to the EEOC, sexual harassment is any type of harassment due to a person's sex that is severe and pervasive and creates a hostile work environment. It can include unwelcome sexual advances and comments of a sexual nature, as well as offensive remarks about a person's sex. Sexual harassment at schools and other educational institutions is also unlawful behavior according to Title IX, passed in 1972.

The following year, a record number of women were elected to Congress. Election year 1992 became known as the "Year of the Woman" when 54 women were elected to Congress.[6] Of those, 47 were in the House and seven in the Senate. These included Carol Moseley Braun, the first black woman senator. The following year, Ruth Bader Ginsberg became the second woman appointed to the Supreme Court.

The Anita Hill–Clarence Thomas controversy also raised awareness about sexual harassment. In the five years after the hearings, the number of people who filed sexual harassment cases with the EEOC more than doubled, going from 6,127 cases in 1991 to 15,342 cases in 1996.[7]

THE THIRD WAVE

Amid the antifeminist backlash and partly in reaction to the Hill-Thomas controversy, a new generation of feminists arose. This part of the women's movement is sometimes referred to as the third wave of feminism. Rebecca Walker coined the term in an essay published by

Ms. magazine in 1992. In the essay, called "Becoming the Third Wave," Walker wrote:

> *Let Thomas' confirmation serve to remind you, as*
> *it did me, that the fight is far from over. Let this*
> *dismissal of a woman's experience move you to anger.*
> *Turn that outrage into political power. . . . I am not*
> *a postfeminist feminist. I am the Third Wave.*[8]

Third wave feminists were seeking to expand the idea of what feminists looked and acted like. In the 1960s and 1970s, second wave feminists had rejected makeup, revealing clothing, and other forms of "objectifying" fashion. Many also shunned the traditional idea of marriage. Their look and lifestyle came to define the movement. As Walker wrote, "For many of us it seems that to be a feminist . . . is to conform to an identity and way of living that doesn't allow for individuality."[9] But in the third wave, Walker contended, feminists no longer had to look or act a certain way. A woman could wear lipstick and high heels if she chose, or have a traditional wedding, and still be considered a feminist.

In addition, the third wave broadened the scope of feminism to include voices of women from different races and classes. It also included lesbian, bisexual, and transgender women. Third wave feminists emphasized the impact of multiple forms of discrimination. Many women of color felt that they had been excluded from the mainstream women's rights movement. Writer bell hooks, the author of *Ain't I a Woman? Black Women and Feminism*, addressed this issue, echoing Sojourner Truth's speech from 1851.

Third wave feminists also found new ways to spread the message of female empowerment. Some female punk rock groups called themselves "riot grrrls." They sang about issues such as domestic abuse, rape, and racism. Magazines known as "grrrl zines" appeared as bold new alternatives to traditional fashion and beauty magazines. They emphasized a strong feminist message and promoted the idea that beauty comes in many colors, shapes, and sizes.

THE MYTH OF BEAUTY

An important third wave feminist issue that still continues today is the problem of female body image. Feeling pressured to look like ultrathin celebrities and fashion models, many girls and women have developed deadly eating disorders and low self-esteem. With their diverse images and empowering message, grrrl zines addressed this problem by creating new definitions of beauty and body.

Naomi Wolf discussed the problem in her 1991 book, *The Beauty Myth*, republished in 2002. She noted, "More women have more money and power and scope and legal recognition than we have ever had before; but in terms of how we feel about ourselves physically, we may actually be worse off than our unliberated grandmothers."[10]

The zines also inspired young women to become politically active and aware.

Today, third wave feminists continue to work in many areas. They address issues such as violence against women, labor issues, and welfare rights. Because of grassroots activism by third wave feminists, Congress passed the Violence Against Women Act (VAWA) in 1994. This federal law provides funds to investigate violent crimes against women. It was reauthorized in 2013. In these and many other ways, third wave feminists helped shape the women's movement as it moved into the new millennium—and beyond. ●

Riot grrrl bands such as Bikini Kill used »
music as a form of feminist protest.

CHAPTER 9

WOMEN'S RIGHTS TODAY AND TOMORROW

Thanks to the women's movement, American women today enjoy freedoms women only dreamed of in 1848. Nobody would think to question women's right to vote, own property, or speak in public. Women today can play sports, attend college, and pursue any careers they choose. Sexism and gender discrimination are banned by law. Female scientists, doctors, lawyers, and politicians are respected in their fields.

In 2012, 40 years after Title IX was instated, more women athletes than men represented the United States at the Olympic Games in London. And more American women brought home gold medals than ever before. The victories testified to the success of Title IX. The law had provided funding for women's sports programs that otherwise might not have existed.

A gap in sports still exists, however. More male than female athletes participate in athletics at both the high school and college level. More female coaches are needed. Men's sports are still more popular with spectators and more financially profitable. Football, played almost

TITLE IX

Title IX is a federal law introduced as part of the Education Amendments of 1972. The law prohibits discrimination based on sex in educational institutions. In the four decades since its passage, Title IX has brought dramatic change. In the 1971–1972 school year, just before Title IX was passed, only approximately 7 percent of high school girls participated in school sports. In 2010–2011, that number had risen to 41 percent.[1] In 1972, just 11 percent of PhDs in the fields of science, engineering, math, and medicine were earned by women. In 2006, women earned 40 percent.[2]

exclusively by men, provides the largest source of revenue for many schools.

But the gains made by Title IX are undeniable. As sports writer Ann Killion stated, "Title IX didn't just provide athletic opportunities to girls, it created a fundamental shift in society, changing perceptions and attitudes and boundaries."[3]

WOMEN IN POLITICS

Women are achieving more in the political arena as well. The number of women at the highest levels of government has continued to climb. Janet Reno became the first female attorney general in 1993 and served until 2001. Between 1996 and 2012, three women—Madeleine Albright, Condoleezza Rice, and Hillary Rodham Clinton—were named secretary of state, the highest-ranking position in the presidential cabinet. In 2007, Nancy Pelosi became the first female Speaker of the House of Representatives. In 2008, Clinton became the first woman to win a presidential primary. In 2009, Sonia Sotomayor became the first Hispanic and the third woman to be appointed to the US Supreme Court. And in 2010, Elena Kagan became the fourth female Supreme Court justice.

In 2000, a record 74 women were elected to Congress—13 senators and 61 representatives. In 2012, that number rose to 97, with 20 in the Senate and 77

VOICES OF THE MOVEMENT

On July 16, 1998, Hillary Rodham Clinton gave a speech at the one hundred fiftieth anniversary of the first women's rights convention at Seneca Falls, linking the movement's past with its future:

❝We cannot . . . ever forget that the rights and opportunities that we enjoy as women today were not just bestowed upon us. . . . They were fought for, agonized over, marched for, jailed for and even died for by brave and persistent women and men who came before us. . . .

Help us imagine a future that keeps faith with the sentiments expressed here in 1848. . . . Each of us can help prepare for that future by doing what we can to speak out for justice and equality, for women's rights and human rights.❞[4]

in the House.[5] Even at these record numbers, women still make up only 18.1 percent of Congress—by far the minority. But according to a *USA Today* report, the increased number of women in leadership positions is likely to change the tone of the nation's government in 2013 and beyond.

THE GLASS CEILING AND THE BRASS CEILING

The "glass ceiling" is a metaphor used to describe the difficulty women have in reaching the highest levels of management in business. Women see these positions right above them, but the "ceiling" blocks women from reaching them. Although they are well represented in middle management, fewer women are able to reach the upper levels. Progress is slow, but the number is rising. In 2013, a record 21 women were listed as chief executive officers of Fortune 500 companies.[6]

Also in 2013, US military officials announced they would lift the ban on women in combat. In the military, experience in combat often leads to higher positions of power. Some feminists believe allowing women to enter combat and special forces units in the military will remove the "brass ceiling" that has prevented them from rising up in the ranks. Women will need to pass rigorous fitness

With the ban on women in combat now lifted, women will have more opportunities to advance in the US military.

tests, as do men, to qualify for these positions. But experts believe women can excel as members of combat units.

A PERSISTENT WAGE GAP

Despite the progress in many areas, women in the United States still struggle with some of the same issues earlier generations faced. One of these continuing issues is the wage gap, or the difference in earnings men make compared to women. Shortly after the 1963 Equal Pay Act was passed, in 1965 women who worked full-time made 59.9 cents for every dollar earned by men. In 1980, they made 60.2 cents to every dollar. In 1999, they made 72.3 cents to men's every dollar.[7]

To help workers address wage gaps, President Barack Obama signed the Lilly Ledbetter Fair Pay Act in 2009. In 1999, Lilly Ledbetter discovered a wage gap that had existed for years at Goodyear Tire and Rubber Company. She sued Goodyear for sexual discrimination. In 2007, her case made it to the Supreme Court. The court ultimately ruled against Ledbetter, citing she should have filed the discrimination charges within 180 days of her first unfair paycheck. But she had not been aware of the wage difference at the time of the first check. The new law bearing her name guarantees that people can sue up to 180 days after any unequal paycheck, not only the first. In a 2012 interview, Ledbetter addressed the personal impact of the wage gap:

> *The first thing that hit me was devastation, humiliation. Then I thought about how many hours of overtime I had worked and not been compensated for what I was legally entitled to, and how hard it had been on my family struggling to pay the*

mortgage, education, doctor bills. We had done without quite a bit. And this was not right.[8]

In 2012, the American Association of University Women (AAUW) released a new study showing that women just one year out of college are paid 82 cents for every dollar paid to their male peers. This is true even when they do the same work and major in the same field. The AAUW report, "Graduating to a Pay Gap," added that overall, women working full-time were earning 77 cents for a man's dollar.[9]

The persistent pay gap is discouraging for women's rights, but the overall trend still shows the gap is gradually decreasing. Women today are also advocating for better health care and day care programs, as these will help working women succeed. Minority women, in particular,

FAMILY DYNAMICS AND THE WAGE GAP

A major piece of the wage gap and glass ceiling seems to be family dynamics. As a 2010 *New York Times* article stated, "Until they have children, young women now earn nearly the same as men and climb the career ladder at a similar pace. With the babies often come career breaks, part-time work and a rushed two-shift existence."[10] Change is slowly happening, however. Family dynamics are shifting. Thanks to the women's movement, no longer are men seen only as the providers and women seen only as the homemakers. Men now often take paternity leave and opt for flexible schedules. These changes can allow both men and women to better balance their careers and their roles as parents.

need help to acquire job skills that will bring them above the poverty line.

WOMEN'S RIGHTS AROUND THE WORLD

Women's rights are an issue all around the world. Significant progress has been made in the international women's movement. In 1979, the United Nations General Assembly adopted a Convention on the Elimination of Discrimination Against Women (CEDAW).
The convention established an international agreement to address women's rights issues around the globe. As of 2011, 187 nations had agreed to be bound by the terms of the treaty.[11]

But more work is needed. One of the goals of the nonprofit organization Human Rights Watch is to empower women internationally. The Alliance for International Women's Rights is another group working for women's rights. This group links professional women in the United States with women in other parts of the world who are looking for tools and resources to improve their lives.

FEMINISTS FOR THE FUTURE

What will feminism of the future look like? Will the women's movement continue? If so, it may not resemble the earlier waves of the women's movement. It may not be centralized around one or two main issues, such as women's suffrage or equal rights in the workplace. And likely, there may not be just one or two leadership figures, such as Susan B. Anthony or Gloria Steinem, representing women's rights in the press and on the political stage.

The Internet and social media continue

to change the way people communicate, including those working for reform. The tools of today—and tomorrow— may allow many different voices and causes to come forth for women. Feminism of the future may not be a large wave, but many ripples of change, spreading all across the world.

TIMELINE

1848 The first women's rights convention is held in Seneca Falls, New York, on July 19.

1850 The first National Women's Rights Convention takes place in Worcester, Massachusetts.

1869 Susan B. Anthony and Elizabeth Cady Stanton form the National Woman Suffrage Association (NWSA).

1890 The NWSA and the American Woman Suffrage Association (AWSA) merge to form the National American Woman Suffrage Association (NAWSA).

1890 Wyoming enters the Union as the first state to grant women suffrage.

1916 Margaret Sanger opens the first birth control clinic in the United States.

1917 Jeannette Rankin of Montana becomes the first woman elected to the US Congress.

1917 Prison guards beat arrested suffragists during the Night of Terror on November 15.

1920 On August 18, the last state, Tennessee, votes to ratify the Nineteenth Amendment to the Constitution, granting women the right to vote.

1933 Frances Perkins, the first woman in a presidential cabinet, serves as secretary of labor.

1963 Betty Friedan publishes *The Feminine Mystique.*

1973 The Supreme Court decision on *Roe v. Wade* legalizes abortion in the United States.

1981 Sandra Day O'Connor becomes the first woman to serve on the US Supreme Court.

1984 Geraldine Ferraro is the first female vice presidential candidate of a major political party.

1992 In the "Year of the Woman," more female candidates are elected to Congress than ever before.

2008 Hillary Rodham Clinton becomes the first female candidate to win a presidential primary.

2009 Sonia Sotomayor becomes the first Hispanic and the third female to be appointed to the US Supreme Court.

WOMEN IN OFFICE: 2013

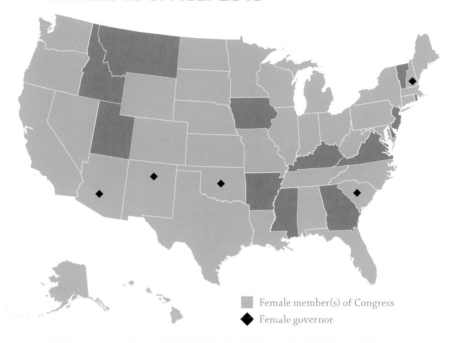

■ Female member(s) of Congress
◆ Female governor

DATE OF THE MOVEMENT'S BEGINNING

1848

LOCATIONS

Seneca Falls, New York; Washington, DC; local protests and events around the country

KEY PLAYERS

Elizabeth Cady Stanton and **Lucretia Mott** organized the 1848 women's rights convention in Seneca Falls, New York.

THE WAGE GAP: 1955–2010

Women's Annual Earnings as a Percent of Men's

Susan B. Anthony worked with Stanton through the second half of the 1800s and was known for her fiery speeches.

Betty Friedan wrote *The Feminine Mystique* in 1963, initiating the second wave of the women's movement.

Journalist **Gloria Steinem** started the feminist magazine *Ms.* and led the movement's second wave.

GOALS AND OUTCOMES

Since the first women's rights convention in Seneca Falls, New York, in 1848, the women's movement has worked for increasingly equal rights for women. The Nineteenth Amendment in 1920 finally granted women the right to vote. Through the 1900s and into the 2000s, the movement has focused on increasing equality in work and wages, ending sex discrimination, and giving women the opportunity to determine their own lives.

GLOSSARY

abolitionist
A person wanting to abolish, or end, slavery.

backlash
A strong reaction against a social or political development.

caucus
A meeting of people from the same political party or group, held to select candidates or decide policy.

conservative
A person who has traditional views about politics, religion, and society that he or she does not want to change.

delegate
A person chosen to represent others at a meeting or convention.

discrimination
Treating a person differently because of the group to which he or she belongs.

lobby
To attempt to change a politician's position on an issue.

militant
A tendency to use activist rather than passive means to achieve goals.

petition
A formal document requesting action.

radical

A person who favors broad, sweeping change or holds views thought to be extreme.

ratify

To approve.

resolution

A goal or statement of intention.

sexism

Discrimination or prejudice based on sex.

suffrage

The right to vote.

ADDITIONAL RESOURCES

SELECTED BIBLIOGRAPHY

Flexner, Eleanor, and Ellen Fitzpatrick. *Century of Struggle: The Women's Rights Movement in the United States.* Cambridge, MA: Harvard UP, 1996. Print.

Friedan, Betty. *The Feminine Mystique.* 1963. New York: Norton, 2001. Print.

Stanton, Elizabeth Cady. *Eighty Years and More: Reminiscences, 1815–1897.* New York: Humanity Books, 2002. Print.

Ward, Geoffrey C., and Ken Burns. *Not for Ourselves Alone.* New York: Knopf, 1999. Print.

FURTHER READINGS

Kamma, Anne. *If You Lived When Women Won Their Rights.* New York: Scholastic, 2006. Print.

Nardo, Don. *The Women's Movement.* Farmington Hills, MI: Lucent, 2011. Print.

WEB SITES

To learn more about the women's rights movement, visit ABDO Publishing Company online at **www.abdopublishing.com**. Web sites about the women's rights movement are featured on our Book Links page. These links are routinely monitored and updated to provide the most current information available.

PLACES TO VISIT

National Susan B. Anthony Museum & House

17 Madison Street
Rochester, NY 14608
585-235-6124
http://www.susanbanthonyhouse.org
The museum features Anthony's artifacts. It also offers
research materials and educational programs.

Wesleyan Chapel,
Women's Rights National Historical Park

Seneca Falls, NY 13148
http://www.nps.gov/wori
Wesleyan Chapel was the location of the first women's rights
convention in 1848. Today it is a historical park offering
tours and more.

SOURCE NOTES

CHAPTER 1. A REVOLUTION BEGINS

1. Eleanor Flexner and Ellen Fitzpatrick. *Century of Struggle: The Women's Rights Movement in the United States.* Cambridge, MA: Harvard UP, 1996. Print. 71.

2. Elizabeth Cady Stanton. *Eighty Years and More: Reminiscences, 1815–1897.* Amherst, NY: Humanity Books, 2002. Print. 20.

3. Ibid. 23.

4. Ibid. 32.

5. "The First Convention Ever Called to Discuss the Civil and Political Rights of Women, Seneca Falls, N.Y., July 19, 20, 1848." *American Memory.* Library of Congress, n.d. Web. 6 May 2013.

6. "Declaration of Sentiments and Resolutions." *The Elizabeth Cady Stanton and Susan B. Anthony Papers.* Rutgers, 1997. Web. 6 May 2013.

7. Ibid.

8. Ibid.

9. Ibid.

10. "The Seneca Falls Convention." *National Portrait Gallery.* Smithsonian Institution, n.d. Web. 6 May 2013.

11. Elisabeth Griffith. *In Her Own Right: The Life of Elizabeth Cady Stanton.* New York: Oxford UP, 1984. Print. 56.

12. Sally G. McMillen. *Seneca Falls and the Origins of the Women's Rights Movement.* New York: Oxford UP, 2008. Print. 93–94.

13. Elisabeth Griffith. *In Her Own Right: The Life of Elizabeth Cady Stanton.* New York: Oxford UP, 1984. Print. 57.

14. Eleanor Flexner and Ellen Fitzpatrick. *Century of Struggle: The Women's Rights Movement in the United States.* Cambridge, MA: Harvard UP, 1996. Print. 77.

15. "*Oneida Whig.* 1 Aug. 1848." *American Treasures of the Library of Congress.* Library of Congress, n.d. Web. 6 May 2013.

16. Elizabeth Cady Stanton, Susan B. Anthony, and Matilda Joslyn Gage, ed. *History of Woman Suffrage.* Vol. 1. New York: Fowler & Wells, 1881. Print. 804.

17. Elizabeth Cady Stanton. *Eighty Years and More: Reminiscences, 1815–1897.* Amherst, NY: Humanity Books, 1993. Print. 149–150.

18. Elisabeth Griffith. *In Her Own Right: The Life of Elizabeth Cady Stanton.* New York: Oxford UP, 1984. Print. 58.

CHAPTER 2. EARLY AMERICAN WOMEN

1. J. K. Hosmer, ed. *John Winthrop's Journal, 1630–1649.* Vol. 2. New York: Scribner's, 1908. Print. 239.

2. "Salem Witch Trials of 1692." *Colonial Gazette.* MayflowerFamilies.com, n.d. Web. 6 May 2013.

3. "Letter from Abigail Adams to John Adams, 31 March–5 April 1776." *Adams Family Papers: An Electronic Archive.* Massachusetts Historical Society, n.d. Web. 6 May 2013.

4. Ibid.

5. Eleanor Flexner and Ellen Fitzpatrick. *Century of Struggle: The Women's Rights Movement in the United States.* Cambridge, MA: Harvard UP, 1996. Print. 36–37.

6. Compton's Interactive Encyclopedia. "Women's History in America." *Women's International Center.* Women's International Center, 1995. Web. 6 May 2013.

CHAPTER 3. A MOVEMENT EMERGES

1. Eleanor Flexner and Ellen Fitzpatrick. *Century of Struggle: The Women's Rights Movement in the United States*. Cambridge, MA: Harvard UP, 1996. Print. 47.

2. Ibid. 91.

3. "Sojourner Truth: 'Ain't I a Woman?', December 1851." *Modern History Sourcebook*. Fordham University, Aug. 1997. Web. 6 May 2013.

4. Elisabeth Griffith. *In Her Own Right: The Life of Elizabeth Cady Stanton*. New York: Oxford UP, 1984. Print. 74.

5. Edith McLaughlin. "The Transformation of Women to Full Participation in the Workforce." *Schmidt Labor Research Center Seminar Paper Series*. University of Rhode Island, 2005. Web. 6 May 2013.

CHAPTER 4. FIGHTING FOR EQUALITY FOR ALL

1. Barbara Wertheimer. *We Were There: The Story of Working Women in America*. New York: Pantheon, 1997. Print. 143.

2. Sally G. McMillen. *Seneca Falls and the Origins of the Women's Rights Movement*. New York: Oxford UP, 2008. Print. 160.

3. Geoffrey C. Ward and Ken Burns. *Not for Ourselves Alone*. New York: Knopf, 1999. Print. 103.

4. "Charters of Freedom: The Constitution of the United States, Amendment XIV." *National Archives*. The US National Archives and Records Administration, n.d. Web. 6 May 2013.

5. "Declaration of Rights of the Women of the United States by the National Woman Suffrage Association." *Claremont Colleges Digital Library*. Claremont University Consortium Records Center, n.d. Web. 6 May 2013.

6. Geoffrey C. Ward and Ken Burns. *Not for Ourselves Alone*. New York: Knopf, 1999. Print. 142.

7. Ibid. 142–143.

8. Ibid. 148.

9. Ibid. 145.

10. Eleanor Flexner and Ellen Fitzpatrick. *Century of Struggle: The Women's Rights Movement in the United States*. Cambridge, MA: Harvard UP, 1996. Print. 153.

11. Geoffrey C. Ward and Ken Burns. *Not for Ourselves Alone*. New York: Knopf, 1999. Print. 149.

CHAPTER 5. GETTING THE VOTE

1. Bolden, Tonya, ed. *33 Things Every Girl Should Know About Women's History*. New York: Crown, 2002. Print. 77.

2. Margaret Sanger. "A Parents' Problem or Woman's?, March 1919." *The Public Writings and Speeches of Margaret Sanger*. Margaret Sanger Papers Project, n.d. Web. 6 May 2013.

3. Geoffrey C. Ward and Ken Burns. *Not for Ourselves Alone*. New York: Knopf, 1999. Print. 188.

4. Lynn Sherr. *Failure Is Impossible: Susan B. Anthony in Her Own Words*. New York, Random House, 1995. Print. 324.

5. Don Nardo. *The Women's Movement*. Farmington Hills, MI: Lucent, 2011. Print. 49.

6. George Sullivan. *The Day the Women Got the Vote: A Photo History of the Women's Rights Movement*. New York: Scholastic, 1994. Print.

7. Eleanor Flexner and Ellen Fitzpatrick. *Century of Struggle: The Women's Rights Movement in the United States.* Cambridge, MA: Harvard UP, 1996. Print. 176.

8. "The Night of Terror, November 15, 1917. Women's Right to Vote." *UCSF National Center of Excellence in Women's Health.* The Regents of the University of California, 6 Feb. 2012. Web. 6 May 2013.

9. "The Movement." *Not for Ourselves Alone: The Story of Elizabeth Cady Stanton and Susan B. Anthony.* PBS, n.d. Web. 6 May 2013.

CHAPTER 6. WOMEN'S CHANGING IMAGE

1. "Jeannette Rankin for Congress." *Legacy.com.* Legacy.com, 8 Mar. 2011. Web. 6 May 2013.

2. "Equal Rights Amendment." *National Organization for Women.* National Organization for Women, n.d. Web. 6 May 2013.

3. "Art, Icons, Women's Rights: 'Rosie The Riveter.'" *The Pop History Dig.* The Pop History Dig, n.d. Web. 6 May 2013.

4. "Table MS-2. Estimated Median Age at First Marriage, by Sex: 1890 to Present." *US Bureau of the Census.* US Bureau of the Census, 15 Sept. 2004. Web. 6 May 2013.

5. Mitra Toosi. "A Century of Change: the US Labor Force, 1950–2050." *Monthly Labor Review Online.* Bureau of Labor Statistics, May 2002. Web. 6 May 2013.

6. Eric Golden. "It's Not 1963, but Women Face Wage Gap." *Omaha.com.* Omaha World Herald, 17 Apr. 2012. Web. 6 May 2013.

7. Betty Friedan. *The Feminine Mystique.* New York: Norton, 2010. Print. 57.

8. David Gergen. "A Candid Conversation with Sandra Day O'Connor: 'I Can Still Make a Difference.'" *Parade.* Parade Publications, 30 Sept. 2012. Web. 6 May 2013.

9. Betty Friedan. *The Feminine Mystique.* New York: Norton, 2010. Print. 64–65.

CHAPTER 7. THE SECOND WAVE

1. "Title VII of the Civil Rights Act of 1964." *US Equal Opportunity Commission.* US Equal Opportunity Commission, n.d. Web. 6 May 2013.

2. "Milestones: 1965." *EEOC 35th Anniversary.* EEOC, n.d. Web. 6 May 2013.

3. Betty Friedan. *The Feminine Mystique.* New York: Norton, 2010. Print. 519.

4. "Highlights from NOW's Forty Fearless Years." *National Organization for Women.* National Organization for Women, 2006. Web. 6 May 2013.

5. "Nation: Women on the March." *Time.* Time, 7 Sept. 1970. Web. 6 May 2013.

6. Carol Hanisch. "The Personal Is Political." *Women of the World, Unite: Writings by Carol Hanisch.* Carol Hanisch, Jan. 2006. Web. 6 May 2013.

7. "Women in Congress." *History, Art & Archives: United States House of the Representatives.* Office of Art & Archives, Office of the Clerk, n.d. Web. 6 May 2013.

8. Susan DeMaggio. "Feminist Gloria Steinem Tells San Diego Audience: We've Come a Huge Distance, but We Still Have a Long Way to Go." *La Jolla Light.* La Jolla Light, 2011. Web. 6 May 2013.

9. Christina Fisanick, ed. *Feminism.* New York: Greenhaven, 2008. Print. 40.

10. "The Equal Rights Amendment." *The Equal Rights Amendment.* The Alice Paul Institute/ERA Task Force of the National Council of Women's Organizations, n.d. Web. 6 May 2013.

11. Roberta W. Francis. "The History Behind the Equal Rights Amendment." *The Equal Rights Amendment.* The Alice Paul Institute/ERA Task Force of the National Council of Women's Organizations, n.d. Web. 6 May 2013.

CHAPTER 8. BACKLASH AND THE THIRD WAVE

1. Stuart A. Kallen. *Women of the 1960s*. Farmington Hills, MI: Lucent, 2003. Print. 84.

2. Douglas Martin. "Obituary: Geraldine Ferraro, 1935–2011: She Ended the Men's Club of National Politics." *New York Times*. New York Times, 27 Mar. 2011. Web. 6 May 2013.

3. Susan Faludi. *Backlash: The Undeclared War against American Women*. New York: Crown, 1991. Print.

4. "Background." *The National Academies Press*. National Academy of Sciences, 2013. Web. 6 May 2013.

5. Jennifer Berry Hawes. "Where is Shannon Faulkner now? First Female Cadet at The Citadel Talks with Oprah Again." *The Post and Courier*. Evening Post Publishing, 20 Oct. 2012. Web. 6 May 2013.

6. "Year of the Woman." *US Senate*. US Senate, n.d. Web. 6 May 2013.

7. "Anita Hill Testifies to Sexual Harassment Against Clarence Thomas." *African American Registry*. African American Registry, 11 Oct. 1991. Web. 6 May 2013.

8. "History." Third Wave Foundation. *Third Wave Foundation*, n.d. Web. 6 May 2013.

9. Rebecca Walker, ed. *To Be Real: Telling the Truth and Changing the Face of Feminism*. New York: Anchor, 1995. Print. xxxiii.

10. Naomi Wolf. *The Beauty Myth*. New York: Harper, 2009. Print. 10.

CHAPTER 9. WOMEN'S RIGHTS TODAY AND TOMORROW

1. "Title IX at 40: Working to Ensure Gender Equity in Education." *National Coalition for Women and Girls in Education*. NCWGE, 2012. Web. 6 May 2013.

2. Ibid.

3. Ann Killion. "Title IX Helped Level Playing Field, Gave Women Chance to Succeed." *SI.com*. Time Warner Company, 2 May 2012. Web. 6 May 2013.

4. Hillary Rodham Clinton. "150th Anniversary of the First Women's Rights Convention." *Congressional Record Online*. Government Printing Office, 27 July 1998. Web. 6 May 2013.

5. "Women in the U.S. House of Representatives 2013." *Center for American Women and Politics*. Rutgers, Apr. 2013. Web. 6 May 2013.

6. Patricia Sellers. "Fortune 500 Women CEOs Hit a Milestone." *CNN Money*. Time Warner, 12 Nov. 2012. Web. 6 May 2013.

7. Ariane Hegewisch, Claudia Williams, and Angela Edwards. "The Gender Wage Gap: 2012." *Institute for Women's Policy Research*. Institute for Women's Policy Research, Mar. 2013. PDF. 6 May 2013.

8. Martha Burk. "Equal Pay: Will We Ever Get There? An Interview with Lilly Ledbetter." *Ms.* Magazine Blog. *Ms.*, 17 Apr. 2012. Web. 6 May 2013.

9. "Graduating to a Pay Gap: The Earnings of Women and Men One Year after College Graduation." *AAUW*. AAUW, 24 Oct. 2012. Web. 6 May 2013.

10. Katrin Bennhold. "Feminism of the Future Relies on Men." *New York Times Europe*. New York Times, 22 June 2010. Web. 6 May 2013.

11. "Convention on the Elimination of All Forms of Discrimination against Women, New York, 18 December 1979." *United Nations Human Rights*. Office of the High Commissioner for Human Rights, n.d. Web. 6 May 2013.

INDEX

ABOUT THE AUTHOR

Jennifer Joline Anderson has been writing since she was a teenager, when she won an award and had a story published in *Seventeen* magazine. She is a graduate of Vassar College, one of the first women's colleges in the United States and coeducational since 1969. She lives in Minneapolis, Minnesota, with her husband, Tim, and three children, Alex, Ruby, and Henry. She writes educational books for young people. Other titles she has written for Abdo Publishing include *The Civil Rights Movement* and *Wilma Rudolph: Track & Field Inspiration.*

ABOUT THE CONSULTANT

Arzoo Osanloo, JD, PhD, is an associate professor at the University of Washington in the Law, Societies, and Justice Program. She is trained in law and anthropology and teaches, conducts research, and lectures on women's and human rights issues.